CRYPTOCURREN CY AND BLOCKCHAIN

UNDERSTANDING THE FUTURE OF MONEY

RICHARD WILLIAMS

Table of contents

INTRODUCTION

In the not-so-distant future, the world experienced a seismic shift in the way people perceived and interacted with money. It was a transformation driven by the rise of cryptocurrencies and their underlying technology, blockchain. What started as a mysterious concept confined to a niche group of tech enthusiasts soon unfolded into a global revolution that forever changed the landscape of finance and economics.

The tale begins with an ambitious young programmer named Sam, who worked tirelessly in a dimly lit apartment, fueled by a passion for decentralized systems. Dissatisfied with the traditional financial institutions that controlled people's money and subjected them to exorbitant fees, Sam set out on a mission to democratize finance.

One fateful evening, as Sam delved into obscure forums and whitepapers, they stumbled upon a revolutionary concept: blockchain. This technology, hailed as the backbone of cryptocurrencies, promised transparency, security, and decentralization. Sam envisioned a world where individuals could control their finances without the interference of banks or governments.

With newfound determination, Sam set to work, developing a groundbreaking cryptocurrency called "LibertyCoin." The concept behind LibertyCoin was simple yet powerful – it empowered individuals to take charge of their financial destiny and participate in a global economy free from intermediaries.

As word spread about LibertyCoin, its popularity skyrocketed, attracting a community of like-minded individuals who believed in the potential of this newfound digital currency. Soon, merchants began to accept LibertyCoin for transactions, and its value surged in the market.

As more people joined the cryptocurrency movement, traditional financial institutions started to take notice. They were initially dismissive, believing cryptocurrencies to be a passing fad. But as LibertyCoin and other cryptocurrencies gained traction, skepticism turned into concern. The old order of finance faced the possibility of being disrupted by this young, digital upstart.

While LibertyCoin flourished, Sam continued to refine the underlying blockchain technology, making it more secure and scalable. The blockchain evolved into a digital ledger of truth, recording every transaction with unwavering accuracy and immutability.

As years passed, governments and regulatory bodies grappled with how to respond to this monetary revolution. Some embraced the idea of digital currencies, recognizing their potential for financial inclusion and economic empowerment. Others remained wary, concerned about potential risks and vulnerabilities in this new landscape.

Through the highs and lows of the cryptocurrency market, one thing became clear – the genie was out of the bottle. The future of money was undergoing a profound transformation, and there was no turning back.

In this unfolding narrative of cryptocurrencies and blockchain, uncertainty and volatility coexisted with hope and progress. The journey was far from over, but one thing was certain – the world would never be the same again, as the enigmatic realm of cryptocurrencies continued to shape the future of money and redefine the way humanity exchanged value.

What are Cryptocurrencies?

Digital forms of money are computerized or virtual monetary standards that utilization cryptography for security and work on decentralized networks, commonly founded on blockchain innovation. Unlike traditional currencies issued and regulated by central authorities, cryptocurrencies rely on a distributed ledger system, which ensures transparency and immutability of transactions.

The most notable digital money is Bitcoin, presented in 2009 by an unknown individual or gathering known as Satoshi Nakamoto. Bitcoin's success paved the way for the emergence of numerous other cryptocurrencies, often referred to as altcoins, such as Ethereum, Ripple, Litecoin, and many more.

One of the key features of cryptocurrencies is their decentralization, which means they are not controlled by any single entity, like a government or a financial institution.

Instead, transactions and consensus are managed by a network of computers through a process known as mining or staking, depending on the underlying protocol.

Cryptocurrencies offer several potential benefits, such as fast and low-cost cross-border transactions, increased financial inclusion for the unbanked, and the potential for privacy and anonymity in transactions. However, they also come with risks, including price volatility, regulatory challenges, and the potential for use in illicit activities.

As the technology and the ecosystem continue to evolve, cryptocurrencies are shaping the future of finance and disrupting traditional systems, opening up new possibilities for decentralized finance (DeFi), non-fungible tokens (NFTs), and other innovative applications.

The Basics of BlockchainTechnology

Blockchain technology is a decentralized and distributed ledger system that forms the foundation of various cryptocurrencies, such as Bitcoin and Ethereum. It operates on a peer-to-peer network, where each participant holds a copy of the entire ledger, ensuring transparency, security, and immutability of data.

At its core, a blockchain consists of blocks, each containing a batch of transactions. These blocks are connected together in sequential request, shaping a chain. The most important aspects of blockchain technology are

1:Decentralization: Unlike traditional centralized systems, blockchain relies on a network of nodes that validate and record transactions, eliminating the need for intermediaries like banks or payment processors.

2:Immutability: Once a transaction is added to a block and confirmed, it cannot be altered or deleted. This makes the blockchain resistant to tampering and fraud.

3:Consensus Mechanism: To maintain the integrity of the ledger, participants must agree on the validity of transactions. Various consensus mechanisms like Proof-of-Work (PoW) and Proof-of-Stake (PoS) are used for this purpose.

4:Security: The cryptographic techniques used in blockchain ensure the security of data and transactions, protecting it from unauthorized access.

5:Transparency: As each exchange is recorded on the blockchain and apparent to all members, it advances straightforwardness and confidence in the framework.

Blockchain technology extends beyond cryptocurrencies and finds applications in various industries like supply chain management, healthcare, finance, and voting systems, among others. Smart contracts, self-executing contracts with predefined conditions, further enhance the capabilities of blockchain by automating processes.

Despite its potential, blockchain technology faces challenges, including scalability, energy consumption (for PoW-based networks), and regulatory issues. However, ongoing research and development aim to address these limitations and unlock the full potential of blockchain for the future.

History of Cryptocurrencies

Cryptocurrencies have rapidly transformed the financial landscape since the introduction of Bitcoin, the first decentralized digital currency, in 2009. This groundbreaking concept marked the beginning of a revolutionary journey that continues to reshape the world of finance. To understand the history of cryptocurrencies, we must delve into the key milestones and developments that have shaped this digital asset class.

The Genesis: Bitcoin

The history of cryptocurrencies traces back to a mysterious figure or group of individuals known as Satoshi Nakamoto, who published the Bitcoin whitepaper in October 2008. In January 2009, the first block of the Bitcoin blockchain, known as the "genesis block," was mined, officially launching Bitcoin. This momentous event marked the beginning of a decentralized and secure digital currency that relied on blockchain technology.

Early Days and Adoption

In the early days, Bitcoin gained popularity among tech enthusiasts and cryptography proponents. The first real-world transaction with Bitcoin took place in 2010 when Laszlo Hanyecz purchased two pizzas for 10,000 Bitcoins, highlighting its potential as a medium of exchange. As more people recognized the value and potential of cryptocurrencies, the demand for Bitcoin grew, leading to the establishment of cryptocurrency exchanges and a broader user base.

Altcoins and Cryptocurrency Diversification

The rise of alternative cryptocurrencies, also known as altcoins, was facilitated by Bitcoin's success. In 2011, Litecoin was introduced, followed by various other cryptocurrencies, each with its unique features and use cases. These digital assets provided an avenue for experimentation and innovation within the blockchain space, leading to the development of various blockchain platforms and smart contract capabilities.

Ethereum and Smart Contracts

In 2015, Ethereum, a decentralized blockchain platform, was launched by Vitalik Buterin. Ethereum introduced the concept of smart contracts, which allowed developers to build decentralized applications (DApps) on top of the blockchain. This breakthrough opened up new possibilities for decentralized finance (DeFi), non-fungible tokens (NFTs), and other decentralized applications.

ICO Boom and Regulatory Challenges

In 2017, the cryptocurrency market experienced a massive surge in value, fueled by the Initial Coin Offering (ICO) boom. ICOs became a popular fundraising method for blockchain projects, but the lack of regulations led to numerous scams and fraudulent activities. Regulators around the world started scrutinizing the cryptocurrency space, leading to the development of more robust regulatory frameworks.

Cryptocurrency Maturation and Institutional Interest

Over the years, cryptocurrencies have matured, and major companies and institutional investors have shown interest in the space. Traditional financial institutions started exploring ways to incorporate cryptocurrencies into their services, and some even began offering crypto-related products to their clients. The increased institutional interest brought more legitimacy to the cryptocurrency market.

Challenges and Scalability

Despite significant progress, cryptocurrencies faced challenges in terms of scalability, transaction speed, and environmental impact. Bitcoin's proof-of-work consensus mechanism consumed substantial energy, raising concerns about its carbon footprint. In response, various cryptocurrencies and blockchain projects started exploring alternative consensus mechanisms, such as proof-of-stake, to reduce their environmental impact.

The Future of Cryptocurrencies

As we look ahead, the future of cryptocurrencies remains promising yet uncertain. They continue to disrupt traditional financial systems, offering borderless and permissionless transactions, financial inclusion for the unbanked, and innovative financial products. However, regulatory hurdles, market volatility, and technological limitations remain key challenges to address for the widespread adoption of cryptocurrencies.

In conclusion, the history of cryptocurrencies has been a journey of innovation, challenges, and breakthroughs. From the creation of Bitcoin as a peer-to-peer electronic cash system to the rise of alternative cryptocurrencies and decentralized applications, the cryptocurrency ecosystem has come a long way. With ongoing developments and growing interest from institutional investors, the future of cryptocurrencies holds immense potential to reshape global finance as we know it.

Early Beginnings and Bitcoin's Genesis

The story of Bitcoin traces back to the early days of the internet and a mysterious figure known as Satoshi Nakamoto. In 2008, Nakamoto published a whitepaper titled "Bitcoin: A Peer-to-Peer Electronic Cash System," introducing the concept of a decentralized digital currency. This marked the beginning of what would become a revolutionary force in the world of finance and technology.

Bitcoin's genesis block, also known as Block 0, was mined on January 3, 2009. This block laid the foundation for the entire blockchain network and contained the famous message "The Times 03/Jan/2009 Chancellor on brink of second bailout for banks." It was a clear statement of the motivation behind creating a system that could operate without the need for traditional financial intermediaries.

Initially, Bitcoin gained traction among technology enthusiasts and early adopters, who saw the potential for a new financial system that could transcend geographical boundaries and be resistant to censorship and manipulation. Over the years, its popularity surged, attracting both praise and skepticism from various quarters.

The decentralized nature of Bitcoin, based on blockchain technology, allowed for secure and transparent transactions. Its scarcity, with a maximum supply of 21 million coins, captured the imagination of investors as a store of value similar to precious metals.

Bitcoin's journey has been marked by price volatility, regulatory challenges, and technological developments. However, it has spurred the growth of an entire ecosystem of cryptocurrencies and blockchain applications, shaping the way we perceive and interact with money and financial systems in the digital age.

In conclusion, the early beginnings of Bitcoin were rooted in a vision to disrupt the traditional financial landscape and usher in a new era of decentralized digital currency. Satoshi Nakamoto's creation sparked a global movement that continues to evolve and shape the future of finance.

Pioneering Altcoins and Development of the Crypto Market

In the early days of cryptocurrencies, Bitcoin was the sole player in the market, acting as the pioneer that introduced the world to blockchain technology and decentralized digital currencies. However, as the crypto community grew, developers and enthusiasts began experimenting with alternative coins, or "altcoins," each offering unique features and use cases beyond Bitcoin's limited capabilities.

One of the earliest altcoins was Litecoin, created in 2011 by Charlie Lee, which aimed to address Bitcoin's scalability issues and offer faster transaction times. This opened the floodgates for other innovative projects like Ripple (XRP), Ethereum (ETH), and many others, each striving to bring something new to the table. Ethereum, in particular, revolutionized the crypto space by introducing smart contracts, enabling developers to build decentralized applications (dApps) on its blockchain.

As the number of altcoins increased, so did the diversity of the crypto market. Traders and investors now had various choices, and the market experienced significant growth. This influx of altcoins also brought attention from institutional investors, governments, and mainstream media, further legitimizing the overall crypto space.

However, the proliferation of altcoins also raised concerns about the potential risks associated with unregulated markets, scams, and volatility. Regulatory challenges became a prominent issue in various jurisdictions as authorities sought to strike a balance between fostering innovation and safeguarding consumers.

Nonetheless, the development of altcoins played a pivotal role in shaping the crypto market into a vibrant ecosystem with a plethora of applications and utility beyond mere financial transactions. Their continued evolution will undoubtedly remain an essential aspect of the crypto landscape as the industry continues to mature and adapt to new challenges and opportunities.

How Cryptocurrencies Work

Cryptocurrencies have revolutionized the financial world since the introduction of Bitcoin in 2009. Operating on decentralized technology called blockchain, cryptocurrencies offer a secure, transparent, and peer-to-peer method of transferring value. To understand how cryptocurrencies work, it's essential to delve into the underlying concepts and mechanisms driving these digital assets.

At the core of cryptocurrencies lies the blockchain, a distributed ledger that records all transactions across a network of computers, or nodes.

A set of transactions and a distinct cryptographic hash link each block to the previous block. This ensures that the entire chain remains tamper-resistant and immutable.

To participate in the cryptocurrency network, users need a digital wallet, which consists of a public address and a private key. The public address acts as an identifier, similar to a bank account number, while the private key is a secret cryptographic code that provides access to the wallet and the funds it holds.

When a user initiates a cryptocurrency transaction, it gets broadcasted to the network and awaits confirmation. Miners or validators, nodes in the network, compete to verify and bundle transactions into a new block. This process involves solving complex mathematical puzzles, and the first miner to solve it gets the right to add the block to the blockchain. As a reward for their efforts and to incentivize the network's security, miners receive newly minted coins and transaction fees.

Once a transaction is confirmed and included in a block, it becomes a permanent part of the blockchain and cannot be altered. This feature ensures transparency and reduces the risk of fraud and double-spending.

In addition to facilitating peer-to-peer transactions, cryptocurrencies can also serve as a means of fundraising through Initial Coin Offerings (ICOs) or Initial Exchange Offerings (IEOs). Projects and companies can issue their own tokens on existing blockchain platforms, allowing investors to buy and hold these tokens as a form of investment or utility within the project's ecosystem.

Despite their numerous advantages, cryptocurrencies face some challenges. The high energy consumption associated with mining and transaction processing has raised concerns about their environmental impact. Moreover, regulatory scrutiny and security vulnerabilities have led to instances of hacks and scams in the cryptocurrency space.

Nonetheless, cryptocurrencies continue to evolve and gain mainstream acceptance. Various industries are exploring blockchain's potential for enhancing security, transparency, and efficiency in supply chains, voting systems, and data management.

In conclusion, cryptocurrencies work through the integration of blockchain technology, which ensures secure and decentralized transactions. They offer an alternative to traditional financial systems, promoting financial inclusion and providing opportunities for innovative applications across different sectors. As this technology progresses, it is crucial to strike a balance between fostering innovation and addressing potential challenges to realize the full potential of cryptocurrencies in the global economy.

Blockchain Explained

Blockchain is a revolutionary technology that underlies cryptocurrencies like Bitcoin, but its applications extend far beyond digital currencies. At its core, a blockchain is a decentralized and distributed ledger that records transactions across a network of computers, creating an immutable and transparent record of information.

The blockchain's strength lies in its security and transparency. Each transaction, or "block," is linked to the previous one through cryptographic hashes, forming a chronological chain. This design prevents tampering, as altering any block would invalidate all subsequent blocks, making it virtually impossible to alter past data.

Decentralization is a key feature of blockchain. Instead of relying on a central authority, the network participants maintain and validate the transactions, ensuring no single entity has control over the entire system. This makes it impervious to restriction and misrepresentation.

Beyond cryptocurrencies, blockchain finds applications in various industries, such as supply chain management, healthcare, finance, and voting systems. It enhances transparency, traceability, and efficiency, saving costs and reducing fraud.

However, blockchain is not without challenges. It faces scalability issues, as each transaction must be verified by all participants. Also, privacy concerns arise when dealing with sensitive data on a public blockchain.

As the technology continues to evolve, developers and businesses explore ways to overcome these limitations, unlocking the full potential of blockchain to revolutionize industries and redefine how we interact with digital information.

Mining and Consensus Mechanisms

Mining and consensus mechanisms are fundamental concepts in blockchain technology, serving as the backbone of decentralized networks. Mining, predominantly associated with proof-of-work (PoW) blockchains like Bitcoin, is the process by which transactions are verified and new blocks are added to the blockchain.

In PoW mining, nodes compete to solve complex mathematical puzzles, and the first one to find the solution gets to add the next block. This requires substantial computational power, making it secure but energy-intensive.

On the other hand, consensus mechanisms like proof-of-stake (PoS) and delegated proof-of-stake (DPoS) aim to address the energy inefficiencies of PoW. In PoS, validators are chosen based on the number of coins they hold and are incentivized to act honestly to avoid losing their staked funds. DPoS introduces a more hierarchical approach, where stakeholders vote for delegates to validate transactions and create new blocks.

Consensus mechanisms are vital for ensuring agreement among network participants, preventing double-spending, and maintaining the integrity of the blockchain. They also influence scalability, security, and decentralization levels of a blockchain network. Different projects may opt for specific mechanisms based on their unique requirements, striking a balance between security, energy consumption, and transaction speed. As the blockchain space evolves, novel consensus mechanisms continue to emerge, fostering innovation and pushing the boundaries of decentralized systems.

Wallets and Security

Wallets play a pivotal role in our daily lives, serving as a repository for our valuable items like money, identification cards, credit cards, and important documents. In the digital age, the concept of wallets has evolved beyond the physical realm to encompass digital wallets used for online transactions and cryptocurrencies. As we increasingly rely on wallets to store sensitive information, ensuring their security becomes paramount.

In the physical realm, traditional wallets can be safeguarded by adopting simple yet effective practices such as keeping them in a secure location, being cautious in crowded areas, and regularly monitoring their contents. However, with the rise of digital wallets, new security challenges emerge. Digital wallets store financial and personal data on mobile devices or online platforms, making them vulnerable to hacking and identity theft.

To enhance the security of digital wallets, various measures have been implemented. Two-factor authentication (2FA) adds an extra layer of protection by requiring a secondary verification method, such as a fingerprint or one-time code. Encryption ensures that sensitive data is converted into unreadable code, making it harder for unauthorized parties to access it. Regular software updates also play a crucial role, as they address vulnerabilities and improve overall security.

For cryptocurrency wallets, the focus shifts to safeguarding private keys, which grant access to the digital assets. Hardware wallets offer enhanced security by keeping the private keys offline and away from potential cyber threats.

In conclusion, whether physical or digital, wallets are essential for securing our valuable belongings. Employing a combination of physical precautions and robust digital security measures is crucial in safeguarding our assets and personal information in the ever-evolving landscape of wallets and security.

Major Cryptocurrencies

Cryptocurrencies have revolutionized the financial landscape, introducing a decentralized and borderless form of digital money. As of my last update in September 2021, several major cryptocurrencies had established themselves as frontrunners in the market. While the landscape is constantly evolving, let's delve into some key players up to that point.

1:Bitcoin (BTC): Launched in 2009 by an anonymous entity known as Satoshi Nakamoto, Bitcoin is the first and most well-known cryptocurrency. As the pioneer of blockchain technology, it operates on a peer-to-peer network and employs a proof-of-work consensus mechanism to validate transactions. Bitcoin's primary use case has been digital gold and a store of value, though some envision it as a future global currency.

2:Ethereum (ETH): Created in 2015 by Vitalik Buterin, Ethereum introduced smart contracts, enabling developers to build decentralized applications (DApps) and tokens on its blockchain. It employs a proof-of-stake mechanism known as Ethereum 2.0, which aims to improve scalability and energy efficiency. Ethereum has become a critical platform for the booming world of decentralized finance (DeFi) and non-fungible tokens (NFTs).

3:Ripple (XRP): Ripple was designed to facilitate fast and cost-effective cross-border payments for financial institutions. Unlike Bitcoin and Ethereum, Ripple's consensus mechanism does not rely on mining but utilizes a unique iterative consensus process. While facing legal challenges from regulatory authorities, Ripple has forged partnerships with major financial institutions.

4:Litecoin (LTC): Launched in 2011 by Charlie Lee, Litecoin is often regarded as the silver to Bitcoin's gold. It is a fork of the Bitcoin codebase but boasts faster transaction times and lower fees due to its different mining algorithm (Scrypt). Though it shares similarities with Bitcoin, Litecoin has its own community and unique value proposition.

5:Bitcoin Cash (BCH): Arising from a contentious hard fork in 2017, Bitcoin Cash sought to address Bitcoin's scalability limitations by increasing the block size. The larger block size allows for more transactions to be processed, potentially reducing transaction fees and increasing transaction speed.

6:Cardano (ADA): Cardano, founded by Charles Hoskinson, is a third-generation blockchain platform that aims to offer scalability, sustainability, and interoperability. It employs a proof-of-stake consensus mechanism and aims to serve as a platform for the development of smart contracts and DApps.

7:Polkadot (DOT): Founded by Gavin Wood, co-founder of Ethereum, Polkadot aims to enable cross-blockchain communication and interoperability. Its unique relay chain architecture facilitates the transfer of data and assets across different blockchains, making it a significant player in the evolving blockchain ecosystem.

It's important to note that the cryptocurrency market is highly volatile and subject to rapid changes. New projects and updates continue to emerge, driving innovation and competition in the space. Before investing or engaging with cryptocurrencies, individuals should conduct thorough research and consider the inherent risks involved.

Bitcoin (BTC)

Bitcoin (BTC) is a revolutionary digital currency and decentralized payment system that emerged in 2009, introduced by an anonymous entity known as Satoshi Nakamoto. It operates on a peer-to-peer network without the need for intermediaries like banks, making it a truly decentralized and transparent system. At the core of Bitcoin's technology is blockchain, a distributed ledger that records all transactions in a secure and immutable manner.

One of Bitcoin's key features is its limited supply, capped at 21 million coins, which creates scarcity and is designed to combat inflation. This scarcity has contributed to Bitcoin's reputation as a store of value and a potential hedge against economic uncertainties. Moreover, its borderless nature allows for quick and low-cost international transactions, appealing to individuals and businesses globally.

However, Bitcoin has faced challenges, including high price volatility, regulatory scrutiny, and environmental concerns due to energy-intensive mining processes. Despite these challenges, it has gained widespread adoption, becoming an investable asset for institutions and a viable payment option for various goods and services.

As the pioneer of cryptocurrencies, Bitcoin has influenced the development of numerous other digital assets, collectively known as altcoins. Its impact on the financial landscape and the ongoing debate over its role in the future of finance continue to shape the world's perception of digital currencies.

Ethereum (ETH)

Ethereum (ETH) is a decentralized blockchain platform and cryptocurrency that revolutionized the world of blockchain technology. Created by Vitalik Buterin in 2015, Ethereum introduced a groundbreaking concept: smart contracts. These self-executing contracts allow developers to build decentralized applications (dApps) on the Ethereum network, enabling a wide range of use cases beyond simple financial transactions.

One of the key strengths of Ethereum lies in its flexibility and programmability. It employs the Ethereum Virtual Machine (EVM), a Turing-complete runtime environment, which enables developers to write complex smart contracts in various programming languages. This has sparked the growth of a vibrant ecosystem with thousands of dApps and tokens deployed on the platform.

ETH, the native cryptocurrency of Ethereum, plays a crucial role in facilitating transactions and powering the network. Miners validate and secure the network by solving complex mathematical puzzles through proof-of-work (PoW) consensus mechanisms, but the network is moving towards a more energy-efficient proof-of-stake (PoS) model with the introduction of Ethereum 2.0.

Ethereum's success has also led to challenges such as scalability and transaction costs, but developers are actively working on solutions like layer-2 protocols and Ethereum upgrades to address these issues. Despite the challenges, Ethereum remains a prominent player in the blockchain space, driving innovation and shaping the decentralized future.

Ripple (XRP)

Ripple (XRP) is a digital asset and cryptocurrency that was created by Ripple Labs in 2012. It is designed to facilitate fast and low-cost cross-border transactions, making it an attractive solution for the financial industry. Unlike traditional blockchain networks, Ripple employs a unique consensus algorithm called the XRP Ledger, which does not require mining and allows for high transaction throughput.

One of the key features of Ripple is its focus on providing real-time settlement capabilities, which can significantly reduce transaction times compared to traditional banking systems. This efficiency has garnered attention from financial institutions, payment processors, and remittance companies, leading to numerous partnerships and integrations.

Critics have raised concerns about the centralized nature of the XRP Ledger, as Ripple Labs holds a significant portion of the XRP supply. However, the company has taken steps to address these concerns and has been working towards decentralizing the network further.

Over the years, Ripple has faced legal challenges from regulators, especially regarding the classification of XRP as a security. These legal issues have impacted its growth and adoption in some regions.

Despite the challenges, Ripple has remained a prominent player in the cryptocurrency space, continually striving to revolutionize cross-border payments and find its place in the ever-evolving world of digital finance.

Litecoin (LTC)

Litecoin (LTC) is a decentralized cryptocurrency that was created in 2011 by Charlie Lee, a former Google engineer. It is often referred to as the "silver to Bitcoin's gold" due to its similarities with Bitcoin and its aim to complement the pioneering cryptocurrency. LTC is based on an open-source blockchain technology, just like Bitcoin, and operates on a proof-of-work consensus mechanism.

One of the main features that set Litecoin apart is its faster block generation time, which is approximately 2.5 minutes, compared to Bitcoin's 10 minutes. This speedier block time takes into account quicker exchange affirmations and better adaptability, making it more appropriate for regular exchanges.

Like many other cryptocurrencies, Litecoin also boasts a limited supply, with a total of 84 million coins that can ever be mined. This scarcity contributes to its value and potential as a store of value.

Throughout its existence, Litecoin has gained a significant following and has been embraced by numerous merchants and businesses worldwide. Its adoption has been driven by its lower transaction fees and wider availability for everyday use.

Despite its success, Litecoin faces competition from other cryptocurrencies and must continuously innovate to maintain its relevance and position in the ever-evolving digital currency landscape. As with any investment, it's essential for individuals to conduct thorough research and exercise caution when considering investing in cryptocurrencies like Litecoin.

Advantages and Disadvantages of Cryptocurrencies

Cryptocurrencies have gained significant attention and popularity in recent years, and they offer several advantages as well as disadvantages. Let's explore these aspects:

Advantages of Cryptocurrencies:

1:Decentralization: One of the vital benefits of cryptographic forms of money is their decentralized nature. They operate on a blockchain, a distributed ledger technology that eliminates the need for central authorities like banks. This decentralization ensures increased security and transparency.

2:Financial Inclusion: Cryptocurrencies have the potential to bring financial services to the unbanked population in developing countries. Individuals without access to traditional banking systems can participate in the global economy by using cryptocurrencies.

3:Low Transaction Fees: Cryptocurrency transactions often have lower fees compared to traditional banking methods. This makes cross-border transactions more cost-effective and efficient.

4:Speed and Accessibility: Traditional banking transfers can take several days, especially for international transactions. Cryptocurrencies enable near-instantaneous transfers, making them ideal for fast-paced financial transactions.

5:Privacy and Security: Cryptocurrencies offer a higher level of privacy for users as transactions are pseudonymous and not directly linked to personal information. Additionally, blockchain technology makes it difficult for malicious actors to tamper with transaction data.

Disadvantages of Cryptocurrencies:

6:Volatility: Cryptocurrencies are notorious for their price volatility. The value of cryptocurrencies can fluctuate dramatically over short periods, leading to potential financial losses for investors and users.

7:Lack of Regulation: The decentralized nature of cryptocurrencies means that they often operate without proper regulation. This can lead to challenges in consumer protection, fraudulent schemes, and potential misuse in illegal activities.

8:Natural Effect: Numerous cryptographic forms of money, like Bitcoin, depend on energy-escalated mining processes. This has raised concerns about their significant carbon footprint, contributing to environmental issues like climate change.

9:Limited Acceptance: While the adoption of cryptocurrencies is growing, they are still not widely accepted as a mainstream form of payment. This limits their practical utility for everyday transactions.

10:Irreversible Transactions: Unlike traditional banking, cryptocurrency transactions are irreversible. In case of accidental errors or fraudulent transactions, it can be challenging to recover funds.

In conclusion, cryptocurrencies offer unique advantages, including decentralization, financial inclusion, and low transaction fees. However, they also come with significant drawbacks, such as price volatility, lack of regulation, and environmental concerns. As the cryptocurrency market continues to evolve, striking a balance between innovation and responsible usage will be crucial for their sustainable integration into the global financial system.

Advantages of Cryptocurrencies

Cryptocurrencies offer various advantages that have transformed the financial landscape. Firstly, they provide enhanced security due to their decentralized nature and cryptographic encryption, reducing the risk of fraud and hacking. Additionally, transactions can be conducted swiftly, enabling fast cross-border transfers without the need for intermediaries like banks, which reduces transaction fees and processing time.

Furthermore, cryptocurrencies empower financial inclusion, offering services to the unbanked population worldwide, fostering economic growth in underserved regions. They also provide transparency, as blockchain technology allows for immutable and traceable transaction records, ensuring accountability and reducing corruption.

Cryptocurrencies enable greater control over personal finances, granting individuals full ownership of their assets without reliance on traditional financial institutions. Moreover, they offer opportunities for investment and diversification, as the market continually evolves with new assets and projects.

Despite these advantages, challenges like price volatility and regulatory uncertainty persist. Nonetheless, the innovative potential of cryptocurrencies continues to inspire various industries and financial systems to adapt and integrate this emerging technology.

Challenges and Risks

Challenges and risks are inherent in various aspects of life, and they play a crucial role in shaping our experiences and decisions. In both personal and professional realms, challenges present opportunities for growth and development. They push individuals and organizations to adapt, innovate, and learn from their experiences. From facing financial hardships to navigating complex relationships, challenges test one's resilience and determination.

Similarly, risks are inevitable when making choices, especially in business and investments. They involve uncertainty and the potential for negative outcomes, ranging from financial losses to reputational damage. However, risks also offer potential rewards and opportunities for success. The key is to assess and manage risks effectively, finding a balance between prudence and ambition.

In the context of technological advancements, challenges and risks have become more complex. Cybersecurity threats, data privacy concerns, and ethical dilemmas are some of the challenges that come with the rapid pace of innovation. Society must address these issues to ensure technology is used responsibly and for the greater good.

Overall, challenges and risks are integral to human existence and progress. Embracing them with a proactive and thoughtful approach allows us to overcome obstacles and navigate uncertain terrain, leading to personal growth, improved decision-making, and the potential for innovation and success.

Blockchain Applications Beyond Cryptocurrencies

Blockchain, originally introduced as the underlying technology behind cryptocurrencies like Bitcoin, has evolved into a transformative force, extending its applications far beyond digital currencies. The decentralized and immutable nature of blockchain offers unique advantages that can be leveraged across various industries, enhancing efficiency, security, and transparency. Here, we explore some of the prominent blockchain applications beyond cryptocurrencies.

1:Supply Chain Management: Blockchain technology has revolutionized supply chain management by providing real-time tracking and traceability of products. Through a distributed ledger, stakeholders can monitor every stage of the supply chain, from raw material sourcing to the final consumer, ensuring authenticity and combating counterfeiting.

2:Healthcare: In the healthcare sector, blockchain enhances data security and interoperability. Patient records stored on a blockchain can be accessed by authorized parties securely, leading to better coordination between healthcare providers and improving patient outcomes. Moreover, blockchain aids in the management of clinical trials and pharmaceutical supply chains, safeguarding drug integrity and reducing fraud.

3:Voting Systems: Blockchain-based voting systems offer a transparent and tamper-resistant alternative to traditional voting methods. Voters can cast their ballots securely, and results can be verified independently, reducing the chances of election fraud and increasing public trust in the democratic process.

4:Intellectual Property: Blockchain enables a decentralized platform for artists, musicians, and creators to protect their intellectual property rights. Smart contracts on the blockchain can automatically enforce copyright rules and ensure fair compensation for content creators when their work is used or shared.

5:Digital Identity Management: Blockchain-based digital identity solutions allow individuals to control their personal information securely. This decentralized approach to identity management minimizes the risk of data breaches and identity theft, providing a safer and more efficient method of identity verification.

6:Energy Management: In the energy sector, blockchain facilitates peer-to-peer energy trading, allowing consumers with solar panels or other renewable energy sources to sell excess energy to others on the network. This decentralized energy market empowers users, promotes renewable energy adoption, and reduces dependence on centralized utility providers.

7:Real Estate: Blockchain streamlines real estate transactions by eliminating intermediaries and reducing paperwork. Smart contracts on the blockchain automate the transfer of property ownership, reducing the time and costs associated with traditional property transfers.

8:Insurance: Blockchain applications in the insurance industry enhance transparency and trust. Through smart contracts, insurers can automate claim settlements, reduce fraudulent claims, and ensure a faster and more efficient claims process.

9:Internet of Things (IoT): Blockchain enhances the security and privacy of IoT devices by enabling decentralized communication and data storage. This mitigates vulnerabilities associated with centralized data storage and prevents unauthorized access to sensitive IoT data.

In conclusion, blockchain technology offers a vast array of applications beyond cryptocurrencies, revolutionizing various industries by providing transparency, security, and efficiency. As the technology continues to evolve, we can expect more innovative use cases to emerge, reshaping the way we interact with data, assets, and each other in the digital world.

Smart Contracts and Decentralized Applications (DApps)

Applications (DApps) are essential pillars of blockchain technology. Smart contracts are self-executing contracts with predefined rules, stored on the blockchain, ensuring transparent, tamper-proof, and automated transactions. They eliminate the need for intermediaries, enhancing security and reducing costs.

Decentralized Applications, or DApps, are applications that run on decentralized networks like Ethereum. They leverage smart contracts to execute tasks without relying on a central authority. DApps have gained popularity due to their transparency, immutability, and resistance to censorship.

The benefits of smart contracts and DApps are numerous. They enable secure peer-to-peer interactions, enabling a wide range of use cases, from decentralized finance (DeFi) and supply chain management to gaming and social networks. However, challenges like scalability, interoperability, and security remain.

As the blockchain ecosystem continues to evolve, smart contracts and DApps will likely play an even more significant role in reshaping various industries and fostering a decentralized future.

Supply Chain Management

Supply Chain Management (SCM) is a crucial discipline that encompasses the coordination and optimization of processes involved in the production, distribution, and delivery of goods and services. It plays a pivotal role in ensuring efficient operations and customer satisfaction.

A well-designed SCM system involves various stages, including sourcing, procurement, production, inventory management, and transportation. By integrating these stages seamlessly, companies can reduce costs, enhance productivity, and minimize disruptions.

In recent years, technology has revolutionized SCM, with the rise of IoT, big data analytics, and artificial intelligence. These innovations enable real-time tracking, demand forecasting, and risk assessment, leading to improved decision-making and adaptability.

Effective supply chain management is not limited to businesses alone. Governments and humanitarian organizations also rely on SCM to deliver aid and resources during emergencies and disasters.

In conclusion, SCM is the backbone of modern commerce, fostering collaboration, efficiency, and resilience across industries, ultimately benefiting consumers and stakeholders alike.

Cryptocurrency Regulation and Legal Landscape

Cryptocurrencies have captured the world's attention since the advent of Bitcoin in 2009. These digital assets offer decentralized and borderless financial transactions, but their disruptive nature has prompted governments to consider implementing regulations to mitigate risks and protect investors. As of my last update in September 2021, the legal landscape surrounding cryptocurrencies was already evolving, and this trend is likely to continue as more countries embrace this new form of finance.

The regulatory approaches toward cryptocurrencies vary significantly across different jurisdictions. Some countries, like Japan and Switzerland, have embraced cryptocurrencies and introduced comprehensive regulatory frameworks to foster innovation while ensuring consumer protection. On the other hand, countries like China have taken a more stringent approach by banning initial coin offerings (ICOs) and imposing restrictions on cryptocurrency exchanges.

One of the key challenges in regulating cryptocurrencies is their inherently global nature. The decentralized nature of blockchain technology allows transactions to occur across borders without intermediaries, making it difficult for individual countries to enforce their regulatory measures effectively. As a result, international cooperation and harmonization of regulations have become essential in addressing issues such as money laundering, fraud, and terrorist financing.

In the United States, the regulatory landscape for cryptocurrencies has been gradually developing. Different agencies, including the Securities and Exchange Commission (SEC) and the Commodity Futures Trading Commission (CFTC), have been actively involved in overseeing aspects of the cryptocurrency market. The classification of cryptocurrencies as securities or commodities remains a complex and evolving topic that affects their regulation and taxation.

European countries have also been exploring ways to regulate cryptocurrencies within the context of the European Union. The EU's Fifth Anti-Money Laundering Directive (AMLD5) brought cryptocurrency exchanges and custodial wallets under its scope, imposing stricter due diligence and reporting requirements. Additionally, the proposed MiCA (Markets in Crypto-assets) regulation aims to provide a comprehensive framework for issuers and service providers in the crypto space.

Developing nations face unique challenges when it comes to cryptocurrency regulation. On one hand, these countries might benefit from the financial inclusion opportunities that cryptocurrencies offer. On the other hand, they must navigate issues related to investor protection, fraud, and the potential for cryptocurrencies to destabilize their existing financial systems.

In conclusion, the regulatory and legal landscape for cryptocurrencies is a constantly evolving domain, shaped by a combination of technological advancements, economic factors, and governmental attitudes. Striking the right balance between fostering innovation and safeguarding consumers remains a complex task for regulators worldwide. As time progresses, international collaboration and adaptability will play crucial roles in creating a conducive and secure environment for the continued growth of cryptocurrencies.

Global Perspectives

Global Perspectives refer to the diverse viewpoints and understandings of issues and events that transcend national boundaries. They encompass political, economic, social, cultural, and environmental dimensions, acknowledging the interconnectedness of our world. Understanding global perspectives is crucial in today's interconnected and interdependent world, where decisions in one region can have far-reaching consequences worldwide.

Embracing global perspectives fosters empathy and open-mindedness, promoting cross-cultural communication and cooperation. It enables individuals and societies to address shared challenges like climate change, poverty, and pandemics collaboratively. Moreover, it encourages critical thinking, as analyzing issues from various angles allows for more comprehensive and informed solutions.

In an era of globalization and rapid technological advancements, being globally aware is no longer a choice but a necessity. By appreciating diverse perspectives, we can work towards a more inclusive, sustainable, and peaceful world, respecting the richness of human experiences and striving for collective progress.

Impact of Regulations on Cryptocurrency Markets

Regulations play a pivotal role in shaping the dynamics of cryptocurrency markets, influencing their growth and stability. On one hand, well-crafted regulations can provide a sense of legitimacy and security to investors, leading to increased adoption and institutional participation in the market. This, in turn, can foster innovation and attract more capital, driving the overall market value higher.

However, poorly designed or excessively restrictive regulations can stifle innovation, hinder market development, and create uncertainty, leading to potential market downturns. The balance between protecting consumers, preventing illicit activities, and fostering innovation remains a challenge for regulators.

Regulatory clarity can also impact the global competitiveness of cryptocurrency markets. Countries with favorable regulations may become attractive hubs for blockchain startups and investments, while others could miss out on potential economic opportunities.

As the cryptocurrency landscape evolves, striking the right balance in regulations becomes crucial to harness the benefits while mitigating potential risks for market participants and the broader financial system.

Cryptocurrency Investment and Trading

Cryptocurrency has emerged as a revolutionary asset class, offering unique opportunities for investment and trading. Unlike traditional fiat currencies, cryptocurrencies are decentralized digital currencies that operate on blockchain technology, enabling secure and transparent transactions worldwide. As the popularity of cryptocurrencies like Bitcoin, Ethereum, and others continues to grow, so does interest in their investment and trading potential.

Investment in cryptocurrencies involves purchasing and holding digital assets with the expectation that their value will increase over time. Many investors see cryptocurrencies as a hedge against inflation and a potential store of value, akin to digital gold. The limited supply and increasing demand for some cryptocurrencies contribute to their price appreciation, making them attractive long-term investment options for those seeking to diversify their portfolios.

Diversification is vital in cryptocurrency investment due to the highly volatile nature of the market. Prices can experience rapid fluctuations, often influenced by news, market sentiment, regulatory developments, and technological advancements. Investors must conduct thorough research, understand the underlying technology, and assess the potential risks before committing capital to this nascent and evolving market.

On the other hand, cryptocurrency trading involves buying and selling digital assets with the aim of profiting from short-term price movements. Traders use various strategies such as day trading, swing trading, and trend following to capitalize on market volatility. Trading can be lucrative, but it also carries higher risks, as the market can be highly unpredictable, and losses can occur rapidly.

To engage in cryptocurrency trading, traders need access to cryptocurrency exchanges, which act as platforms for buying and selling digital assets. These exchanges offer various trading pairs and tools to assist traders in making informed decisions, such as charting tools, order types, and market analysis features.

Both investment and trading in the cryptocurrency market require a solid understanding of market dynamics and risk management principles. Traders and investors should stay updated with market news, analyze price trends, and adopt suitable risk management strategies to protect their capital.

Regulation is another important consideration when investing or trading cryptocurrencies. Regulatory environments differ from one country to another, and new regulations can impact market sentiment and price movements. Understanding and complying with relevant regulations is crucial to mitigate potential risks and uncertainties.

In conclusion, cryptocurrency investment and trading present unique opportunities for investors and traders to participate in the ever-evolving digital

economy. While investment offers long-term potential for
portfolio diversification, trading can provide opportunities for short-term profits. However, the cryptocurrency market's volatility and lack of regulation require careful research, risk management, and an understanding that the potential for gains is accompanied by potential for losses. As the industry continues to mature, both investment and trading in cryptocurrencies remain a subject of significant interest and debate among financial professionals and enthusiasts alike.

Understanding Market Trends

Understanding market trends is a crucial aspect of any business's success. Market trends refer to the patterns, behaviors, and shifts in the market that influence consumer preferences, demand, and overall business performance. By analyzing market trends, companies can identify opportunities, anticipate challenges, and make informed decisions.

To comprehend market trends, businesses must conduct thorough market research, gathering data on customer preferences, competitor strategies, economic indicators, and technological advancements. Analyzing this data helps in spotting emerging trends and understanding consumer needs.

Staying updated on market trends enables businesses to adapt their products, services, and marketing strategies accordingly. For instance, with the rise of e-commerce, companies need to incorporate online sales channels to remain competitive. Similarly, changes in consumer preferences towards eco-friendly products necessitate sustainable practices and offerings.

Continuous monitoring of market trends empowers businesses to be proactive rather than reactive. Anticipating market shifts allows them to plan ahead, reduce risks, and seize opportunities swiftly. Embracing innovation and technology, such as data analytics and AI, can aid in this process.

In conclusion, understanding market trends is the foundation for strategic decision-making and sustainable growth. Businesses that prioritize market analysis and adapt to changing dynamics are better positioned to thrive in today's dynamic and ever-evolving marketplace.

Tips for Secure Trading

Secure trading is essential for protecting your assets and personal information during online transactions. Here are some valuable tips to ensure a safe trading experience:

1:Research: Thoroughly investigate the trading platform or website before initiating any transactions. Look for user reviews, security certifications, and the platform's history.

2:Strong Passwords: Create unique and complex passwords for your trading accounts, avoiding easily guessable information.

3:Two-Variable   Confirmation:
Empower two-factor verification at
whatever point conceivable to add an
additional layer of safety to your
records.

4:Beware of Phishing: Be cautious of
emails or messages asking for sensitive
information, and never click on
suspicious links.

5:Secure Network: Trade on secure
and private networks, avoiding public
Wi-Fi or untrusted connections.

6:Regular Updates: Keep your trading
platform and devices up-to-date with the
latest security patches.

7:Diversify Funds: Avoid keeping all
your funds in one trading account;
diversify across multiple platforms.

8:Use Licensed Brokers: Trade with
reputable and licensed brokers to
reduce the risk of fraudulent activities.

By following these tips, you can
minimize the chances of falling victim to
cyber threats and ensure secure trading
practices.

Investment Strategies

Investment strategies are essential
plans and approaches adopted by
individuals or organizations to manage
their finances and achieve specific
financial goals. There are numerous
investment strategies, each catering to
different risk appetites, time horizons,
and objectives. Some common
strategies include:

1:Buy and Hold: Investors purchase
assets with a long-term view, aiming to
benefit from market growth over time.

2:Diversification: Spreading
investments across various assets to

reduce risk and minimize the impact of potential losses.

3:Dollar-Cost Averaging: Investing a fixed amount at regular intervals to take advantage of market fluctuations and average out purchase prices.

Value Investing: Seeking undervalued assets with strong fundamentals to hold until their true value is recognized.

4:Growth Investing: Focusing on assets with high growth potential, often in emerging industries or companies.

5:Income Investing: Prioritizing assets that generate regular income, such as dividends or interest.

Choosing the right investment strategy depends on individual financial goals, risk tolerance, and time horizon. Regularly reviewing and adjusting strategies based on changing market conditions is crucial for successful investment management.

The Future of Cryptocurrencies and Blockchain Technology

Cryptocurrencies and blockchain technology have rapidly evolved since the inception of Bitcoin in 2009. Over the years, they have transformed the financial landscape and disrupted traditional industries. As we look into the future, it is evident that cryptocurrencies and blockchain will continue to play a pivotal role in shaping various sectors.

One of the most prominent aspects of the future of cryptocurrencies is their mainstream adoption. As governments and institutions recognize their potential, they are gradually integrating them into their financial systems. Central bank digital currencies (CBDCs) are being explored by several countries, enabling them to leverage blockchain technology while retaining control over their monetary policies. This move towards digital currencies fosters financial inclusion and reduces transaction costs, making cross-border payments faster and cheaper.

Furthermore, as regulatory frameworks become clearer, more investors and institutions will enter the cryptocurrency market, driving its maturation. This increased participation will likely lead to greater stability, reduced volatility, and enhanced liquidity. Additionally, the integration of cryptocurrencies into traditional financial systems could lead to the blurring of lines between traditional finance and decentralized finance (DeFi). DeFi platforms, powered by blockchain technology, offer various financial services, including lending, borrowing, and yield farming, without intermediaries. The future may see these decentralized platforms competing with traditional financial institutions, challenging the existing financial infrastructure.

Interoperability will also be a significant development in the future of blockchain technology. Currently, there are numerous blockchain networks, each with its own protocols and ecosystems. Efforts to create cross-chain compatibility, such as blockchain bridges and inter-chain communication protocols, will enable seamless data and asset transfer between different blockchains. This will foster greater collaboration, efficiency, and scalability in the decentralized ecosystem.

Moreover, the future will likely witness an evolution in the use cases of blockchain technology beyond finance. Industries like supply chain management, healthcare, energy, and real estate are exploring blockchain applications to enhance transparency, security, and traceability. The tamper-resistant nature of blockchain ensures the integrity of data, reducing fraud and improving the overall efficiency of various processes.

However, with greater adoption and innovation comes the challenge of scaling blockchain networks to accommodate the growing user base and transaction volume. Several projects are actively working on improving blockchain scalability through techniques like sharding, layer-two solutions, and proof-of-stake consensus algorithms. Overcoming these scalability hurdles will be essential to support mass adoption and the seamless integration of blockchain into our daily lives.

In conclusion, the future of cryptocurrencies and blockchain technology is promising, with the potential to revolutionize industries, improve financial inclusivity, and provide secure, transparent solutions. Mainstream adoption, regulatory clarity, and technological advancements will drive this transformation, making cryptocurrencies and blockchain an integral part of our future global economy.

Integration with Traditional Financial Systems

Integration with traditional financial systems refers to the incorporation of modern technology and digital platforms into existing financial infrastructures. This convergence allows for seamless interactions between conventional banking systems and fintech solutions, creating a more efficient and user-friendly experience.

By integrating with traditional financial systems, fintech companies can access a broader customer base and offer innovative services. Mobile payment apps, peer-to-peer lending platforms, and digital wallets are examples of such solutions that have revolutionized the financial landscape.

Furthermore, this integration enables better risk management, regulatory compliance, and security measures, fostering trust among users and institutions. It also streamlines processes, reducing costs and increasing accessibility, especially for underserved populations.

Nonetheless, integrating with traditional systems requires careful coordination and adherence to regulatory frameworks. Collaboration between fintech startups and established financial institutions becomes crucial to ensure a successful fusion of old and new technologies, ultimately benefiting consumers with enhanced financial services and experiences.

Challenges and Opportunities Ahead

As we look ahead, the world is filled with both challenges and opportunities. One of the significant challenges we face is the global climate crisis, requiring urgent action to mitigate its devastating effects. Moreover, the digital revolution brings challenges of cybersecurity and data privacy, demanding robust solutions to safeguard sensitive information.

However, amidst these challenges lie tremendous opportunities. Technological advancements, like artificial intelligence and renewable energy, offer transformative solutions to address pressing issues. Embracing sustainable practices can pave the way for a greener, more resilient future. Furthermore, the growing interconnectedness of the world creates opportunities for international cooperation and collaborative problem-solving.

Education plays a pivotal role in shaping the future, equipping the next generation with the skills needed to navigate these challenges and harness opportunities. Emphasizing inclusivity and diversity can lead to innovative breakthroughs and a more harmonious global community. By tackling challenges head-on and seizing opportunities, we can build a brighter and more prosperous future for all.

Conclusion

In conclusion, the emergence of cryptocurrencies and blockchain technology has heralded a transformative shift in the world of finance and the broader concept of money. Cryptocurrencies, such as Bitcoin, Ethereum, and others, have challenged the traditional financial system by offering decentralized, transparent, and secure alternatives for transactions and wealth storage. Their underlying technology, blockchain, serves as a revolutionary digital ledger, enabling trustless and immutable record-keeping across various industries.

As we move forward, it becomes increasingly evident that cryptocurrencies and blockchain have the potential to redefine the future of money. Their disruptive nature has garnered widespread attention from individuals, businesses, and governments worldwide. The decentralization aspect of cryptocurrencies empowers people by providing financial access to the unbanked and underserved populations, fostering financial inclusion on a global scale.

Furthermore, blockchain technology's potential extends beyond financial applications, with numerous sectors exploring its capabilities, including supply chain management, healthcare, real estate, and more. The concept of smart contracts embedded within blockchains promises to revolutionize contract execution, streamlining processes and minimizing disputes.

However, as with any emerging technology, there are challenges to overcome, including regulatory concerns, scalability issues, and environmental impacts associated with energy-intensive mining processes. Collaboration between governments, industries, and innovators will be vital in addressing these challenges and unlocking the full potential of cryptocurrencies and blockchain.

In conclusion, the future of money undoubtedly involves cryptocurrencies and blockchain technology. As these technologies continue to evolve and mature, they have the potential to reshape our financial landscape, promoting inclusivity, efficiency, and transparency in ways we have yet to fully comprehend. Embracing and responsibly harnessing the power of these transformative technologies will be key to unlocking a brighter financial future for the world.

www.ingramcontent.com/pod-product-compliance
Lightning Source LLC
Chambersburg PA
CBHW061053050326
40690CB00012B/2606